THE MAN CODE

A WOMAN'S GUIDE TO CRACKING THE TOUGH GUY

By David Good

Edited by Scott Brown
Design by Barb Hennelly, Romp Creative
Photography by Colin Vincent

Imagine Media, LLC
San Francisco • Portland

2010 Imagine Media Trade Paperback Edition
Copyright © 2010 by David Good
All rights reserved
Published in the United States by Imagine Media, LLC
Imagine Media is a trademark of Imagine Media, LLC

Library of Congress Cataloging-in-Publication data
Good, David
The Man Code
A Woman's Guide To Cracking The Tough Guy
By David Good
ISBN: 098433634-6

Printed in the United States of America
www.mancodebook.com

Edited by Scott Brown
Book design by Romp Creative
Website design by Romp Creative
Photography by Colin Vincent

DEDICATION

For my mother and father. Thank you for always being there for me. It's only as I get older that I realize how unbelievable you two both were and are.

Mom—the love you showed and what you did as a single mother day in and day out is mind-boggling to me. As the years go by, I understand more fully how hard that must have been for you and the sacrifices you made for us. Thank you.

Dad—some kids have Spiderman or Batman, but since the day I was born you have been my hero. You remain the hardest-working person I have ever met and probably ever will. You truly set the bar for what a man's man is. My only hope is I can turn out to be half the father you are to me. Thank you.

There was never a time when I did not feel unconditionally loved and supported by you both. That love and support for me is the reason I have been able to take so many chances in life, as I know deep down that even if I fail I still have you two there to pick me up. *Thank you.*

ACKNOWLEDGEMENTS

I want to thank my stepparents, grandparents, aunts, uncles, sisters, cousins, coaches, teachers, friends, and everyone else who played a role in instilling the values that helped me develop into what I hope is a Man Code man.

I want to thank ABC for the incredible opportunities they've afforded me, and for giving me the platform to find an audience for this book. Thank you to my castmates on "The Bachelorette" and "Bachelor Pad," especially my partners in crime, Jesse Kovacs and Natalie Getz.

Thank you to the talented team that made this book possible, including Scott Brown, Neal Rosenshein and Dusty Schmidt from Imagine Media; Barb Hennelly and Jake Favour with Romp Creative; Inna Shamis with AvantGarde Communications Group; and the very talented photographer Colin Vincent.

There are too many friends to name from my homes in Ohio and Florida, and all parts in between. Suffice it to say the list is long. A special nod to the gang at The Slug, where I was "discovered" and continue to spend some of my most productive hours.

TABLE OF CONTENTS

MAN CODE [man-kohd] man·code —noun.
The Man Code is an unwritten code of conduct that guides the standard to which a man holds other men and himself. It governs masculinity, and dictates the way men treat the women in their lives. Understanding the code empowers women to request and receive more from their men than was previously possible.

INTRODUCTION

I understand why you'd be dubious.

I'm not a psychologist, nor am I a sociologist, and therefore must lack the pedigree necessary to define the dynamic between men and women in the 21st century. Put more bluntly, on the surface this book might be interpreted as a reality TV personality who's overshot his mark in hoping to extend his 15 minutes of fame.

I understand that perception. I'm just a guy from small-town Ohio—I don't pretend to be versed in the ways of the world.

But there is one thing on which I am an expert: guy's guys. Men's men. Hardened dudes with soft centers and dirt under their fingernails. The sort of guys who are the subjects of Hank Williams songs. I've been immersed in masculine energy since the day I was born, and understand the species from top to bottom.

In other words, I've got a doctorate in Man Code. Just as no one knows more about crime than a criminal, I'm confident no one knows more about how men operate than I do.

My field research consists of nearly 30 years spent living in America's heartland. The region where I'm from consists of small towns strung together like pearls by an open highway, with nothing but farmland as far as the eye can see. We don't have a scenic coast or beautiful mountain ranges to distinguish us. The sum total of the beauty in our towns belongs to those who live in them.

Guys there are bound by a common ethic that presents itself in our work, our friendships and our romantic relationships. That ethic is honesty, and it differentiates Man Code men from bad boys, frat boys and metrosexuals, to name just a few alternate species.

The fact is, long before I was on television, I'd spoken with my dad about publishing a book like "The Man Code." As co-winner on the ABC show "Bachelor Pad," I now have the platform to find an audience.

My dad and I agreed that manliness is at a crossroads in our culture. There are fewer and fewer men like the ones I grew up with, a fact you can attribute to any combination of divorce, technology and the decline of blue-collar labor in America. To some extent I wanted to plant a flag in this moment and offer some kind of treatise on masculinity.

I had another motivation in writing "The Man Code." It's safe to say that my buddies and I want to have love in our lives just as much as the next guy. Unfortunately, we are a uniquely impenetrable group. Why? Let me count the ways...

WHY IT'S HARD TO CRACK
A MAN CODE GUY

1. We're pack animals and therefore confused by one-on-one intimacy.

2. We're literal-minded and therefore don't pick up on subtlety.

3. We refuse to pay women the compliment of asking for their help.

4. We're not the greatest listeners, especially when stories take longer than 30 seconds to tell.

5. Our friends are idiots because...they just are.

6. We're overly principled and resist being where we have to be when we don't want to be there, and we hate saying what we have to say when we don't mean it.

7. The act of telling us about your problem while not wanting us to actually fix the problem is totally baffling.

8. We move far more slowly and refuse to take chances on love because it clashes with our protective instinct to do so.

9. We are emotional camels, conserving every kind word and providing too-infrequent validation of the way we feel about you.

(This list is the abbreviated version. Summary: we make it very hard for you to understand and love us.)

But here's the thing: if I was giving my sister advice, I would tell her to settle for no one but a Man Code man. I honestly believe the Man Code represents the best subset of the American male, and I'll defend that point throughout this book. Not only am I scared the Man Code man is becoming endangered, I'm also saddened by the fact that those who do exist find themselves continually frustrated when it comes to love.

That brings us to my second reason for writing this book: romance. To an extent I'm playing matchmaker. My buddies are great people, yet too many of them go home to an empty house because women find them too difficult to understand. The fact is, we're simple creatures; the supposed complexity of the Man Code man is something women project on us.

I'm pulling back the veil and lifting up the hood of the Man Code, an unspoken set of rules that govern masculinity. Hopefully this will shed some light on the soft spot that exists deep inside these guy's guys, allowing love to flourish.

I think my playing matchmaker here has something to do with my parents' divorce when I was 9. I remember sitting at the top of the steps crying as they fought over money, my dad's long hours...you name it. Once we moved out, I remember worrying about my dad being alone in that big house. I remember being furious with my mother for not loving him anymore. My dad is a Grade A man's man, and though he felt he was doing the right things for our family, it just came out wrong. I can't help but feel that a little introspection like what you'll find in this book could have gone a long way toward them establishing an understanding.

This book does not promise you what a lot of women's magazines do on their covers: the secret to luring bad boys into your lair and under your influence. This sort of advice presumes that a woman should change who she is in order to get a man. To me, this is disempowering, and what I want to do here is empower. I'm not telling you how to please us or coerce us. I just want to help you understand us. Where you take it from there is up to you. How are men and women different? My point is not to illustrate this, but simply to explain men the best I can—and not all men, but just one kind of man. If you're reading this book, chances are that you love or have loved a person who'd fall under the category of "tough guy" or "man's man."

"The Man Code" is not about "bros before ho's," nor is it a punch list to be sent around via email: Rule #8—No two men should share an umbrella. Rule #23: Any man who hooks up with a friend's sister does so at the peril of his own life. This isn't "Entourage" explained. It's not "bro code." This book is for women, and about men. Real men.

Finally, I wrote this book to set the record straight as to the true Man Code. The Code is really important to me because it's something I learned from my dad. But when I first brought it up on national television—during my appearance on "The Bachelorette" (Jillian's season)—I was behaving badly and acting as though I had no code of conduct at all. I confronted Juan, a guy in the house, in a very ugly way, and later went in for a kiss with Jillian when she didn't want one. My language overall was terrible. When I returned home, I apologized to those closest to me for the way I acted.

What caused my behavior? I'd say some combination of immaturity, testosterone, alcohol and boredom. Later in this book, I explain the context in which those things occurred. You won't be surprised to learn that I feel I was given a pretty bad edit, and that had the viewer been in the house with us, they'd have seen those events differently. But compressing time is the name of the game on those shows, and I provided the ammunition for my portrayal. Part of my goal in going back on "Bachelor Pad" was to show the man I knew I could be, and to represent the Man Code for all it truly means. I feel like I did that.

I hope you can tell I've thought a lot about this stuff, and if this is my 15 minutes' last gasp, I want to make it mean something. In short, "The Man Code" is about insisting on a man who exhibits pride, chivalry, and respect. It's also about finding true happiness with a guy who's a man among men.

David Good

WHERE I LEARNED
THE MAN CODE

The story goes that the way to a man's heart is through his stomach. Presuming that's correct, my road begins with McDonald's and a cinnamon roll.

Before I was school age, my dad used to come into my room at 3 a.m. and say, "C'mon, bud. Get up. Let's go."

My dad eventually went on to build a successful warehousing business near Dayton. But back then he drove a truck. Twice a day he'd haul cement from near our home in West Alexandria, Ohio, to a yard in Dundee, Michigan. Each leg of the drive took roughly three hours, and he brought me along for company.

I usually slept in the cab for the first session, waking up in Dundee to the smell of a McDonald's breakfast and a cinnamon roll. Dundee is a village of about 3,500 people. But it was like Manhattan to a roughneck boy who didn't know any better, with its hulking factories and enormous water towers. They call Dundee the "Hub of the Highways" because it's essentially an intersection where truckers like my dad converge.

God, how I loved those trucks. I used to get down underneath them, smear grease all over my face, hand my dad wrenches and pretend that I was working on their transmissions. I probably got in the way more than anything but my dad encouraged my help nonetheless. On the drive home, I'd talk on the CB radio, and we'd play games where the first one to spot a blue Peterbilt truck or a car with one headlight would be the big winner.

We didn't have much back then, not unlike many of the 1,500 that constitute West Alexandria's population. Initially we lived with another family until my parents saved enough to rent a farmhouse up the road. It was surrounded by 150 acres of farmland, and I promise you I explored every square foot. The nearest house was a half-mile away. It was boy heaven.

I was given real responsibility around the house from an early age, including feeding pigs and sheep, as well as mowing five acres on a Farmall Cub tractor when I was only seven. By age 12 I was working summers for another farmer, baling straw 15 hours a day. My dad would drop me off on his way to work and pick me up on his way back. I drove my first semi-trailer when I was 14, following my dad along eight miles of dark road. When I turned 16 I immediately started illegally hauling steel loads for 20 miles down Highway 35.

I don't think I'm necessarily unique in this. A common denominator among Man Code men is the work ethic we were taught early on. In fact, I think we look back at the hard work we were made to do and remember it almost romantically. That foundation is the one on which a Man Code man stands. We think, "Work first. Play second." We won't relent until our responsibilities are tended to.

Everything we did on those drives was manly. We hauled bulls around for the rodeo. In fact, one time we were driving cattle to Cincinnati and the trailer gate swung wide open, scattering cattle all over the highway. Soon they were eating grass in an old lady's yard, with us trying to prod them back into the trailer.

Another time, we were hit by a tornado, which ripped the trailer right off the hitch, spinning it 50 feet into the air before it set down in the middle of a cornfield, standing perfectly upright and unharmed.

Regardless of the adventure being real or just something we'd imagine to pass the time, I knew I was special because my dad picked me to spend 12 hours with every day. When school started, I'd hear his engine start at 3 in the morning and I'd spring from bed, pressing my nose up against the window and wishing I could go with him.

It was my dad who taught me there was no easy route to success. "Just because something is easy," he'd say, "doesn't make it right. If you want a better life, you'll have to take the dirt road from here to there." Many kids emerge from their childhoods feeling entitled. That was not the case with me.

Just like iron sharpens iron, men sharpen other men. It's how our character gets honed; it's how we develop a unique language with one another. (This is, in part, why we have such a difficult time communicating our feelings to women—so often it seems they're speaking an entirely different language. Ladies, have you ever tried talking to your dog, and all it does is tilt its head quizzically? It's pretty much the same thing for humans, with men playing the role of the dog.) Iron must be in the presence of iron in order to become refined, and men need other men for that same reason. The process of sharpening my character started with my dad.

The Man Code is learned, not taught, and my education began on the road to Dundee.

You've never seen a man with drive like my father's. I watched him build a $7 million company from scratch. If the competition was working 12-hour days, he'd work 13. I had a front row-seat for every drop of blood, every bead of sweat, and every tear he shed building that company—with an emphasis on the tears.

My parents divorced when I was nine, an event largely attributable to his complete immersion in work. No matter how many times he said he was working so hard for us, nothing could make up for the 100-hour weeks he spent away from the family. I can remember him leaving and saying to me, "You're the man of the house now. Look out for your sister, and hold doors open for your mom. Can you do that?"

I'll pause here and say that a convergence of events gave me an in-depth understanding of Man Code, and as critical as my dad's example was, my mother's was equally significant. It would literally be impossible to be raised by my mother and not hold women in anything but the highest regard.

I'd understand if you thought subscribers to the Man Code are the sorts who view the 1960s as the apex for men, who had dominance and control before women's lib, civil rights and political correctness took hold. But believe it or not, "Mad Men's" Don Draper—the epitome of power and gratification—is not a Man Code man. Not if I have a vote.

To me, a Man Code man is chivalrous and seeks a woman who is his partner 50/50 in every respect. We just have a hard time expressing this, and naturally you mistake our grunts and/or silence as dissatisfaction.

All of this said, the one issue my eventual wife will have to contend with the most will likely be my instinct to provide and protect, which I translate into "work, work and work some more." Finding sea level where everyone is happy will undoubtedly take a little trial and error.

I can still remember my parents fighting. I'd sit at the top of the stairs crying, listening to them argue until 2 a.m., oftentimes about money and dad's long hours at work. When my folks divorced, we went to live with my grandparents, leaving my father to fend for himself in that huge farmhouse, with a single towering farm light shining down on it.

I think that was when my protective instinct kicked in, and ironically it was directed at my dad. I worried about him being completely alone in that house, surrounded by 150 acres of oblivion. Even today, I tear up at the thought of him coming home to nothing but quiet and darkness.

The first year, I only got to see him every other weekend—no more trips to Dundee. Parting was horrifying. I'd cry, my sister would cry, he would cry, my mom would cry. I was furious with my mother: Why couldn't she love my dad anymore? "I still do love him," she reassured me. "We just can't live together."

I'm not unique in this experience. Nearly two-thirds of my peers were raised in broken homes. I can't speak for the impact this has on young women, but I can say confidently that the divorce epidemic has resulted in a generation of extremely guarded men. I get into this more in subsequent chapters, but the heaviness of divorce, combined with an entire demographic raised without a man in the house on a daily basis, has us either deflecting love or putting our needs ahead of our partners'. The concept of giving pleasure to get pleasure is entirely lost on many of my peers, and I fear it has Man Code men on the wane.

I was fortunate in that my mother correctly identified I had a lot of my father in me. Without a change of course I'd end up in the same sort of marriage they had, with real love squandered by a bottomless sense of responsibility and competitive drive. After all, day in and day out, I was the high school basketball player waiting for the gym to open at 5 a.m., to the extent that when I graduated our school janitor wrote me a letter saying how much she admired my determination. I was the jock who thought to himself, "I better be kind to everyone in this school, because some day they'll be working for me." I was the guy who willed himself to become a Division I football player, walking on at University of Miami–Ohio and starting as a freshman on all four special teams, playing in front of 100,000 screaming fans (including my weeping parents) at University of Michigan. I was the guy who, when all my friends were getting married and having kids in their early 20s, moved to Tampa to work for one of the fastest growing truckload freight brokers in the United States. To a community where thoughts of simply leaving Preble County were grandiose, I was an astronaut.

But I was something else, too. Had my mother not intervened, I was my father waiting to happen.

She was obviously not pleased with the way things went in her marriage, and she'd be damned if they were to be replicated in my life. She would not let divorce beget divorce in my instance.

My father taught me how to work; my mother taught me how to be in this world. She preached to me that work is not everything. She taught me that being with a woman means more than just sex. It means spending time, complimenting and cherishing. She said I shouldn't expect anything from a woman, including cooking, cleaning and laundry. I had to learn to do those things for myself.

No point went uncovered, even the obvious ones like, "Girls are not like guys. You can't make fun of them when they cry."

My mom went to work at the local newspaper soon after she split with my dad. Though I didn't know it at the time, I look back now and realize my mom was Superwoman. She didn't complain; she just picked herself up, dusted herself off and never faltered. At my high school graduation my cousin Bill, who lived just down the street from us, came up and said, "I'm so impressed with what your mom did for you guys." That's when it sank in.

I was raised in a place where men are blue collar in one form or another, where they take pride in their community and country, and where they mostly grow up to imitate the life their father led before them. A man dignifies himself by working, and let anyone who didn't feel the same be damned. Whether you were enjoying life or enduring it, the expression on your face should remain the same.

Until I got to college, I thought the rest of the masculine world must subscribe to this same simple code. It was only then that I got a glimpse of a world without a Man Code. I couldn't believe the lack of humility. I rolled up to my dorm in a beat up '78 Camaro I'd rebuilt myself, trying to find a place to park amid a field of BMWs. It dawned on me that my family never had very much money, though I never knew it. My dad drove a beat-up Dodge pickup; my mother had a four-door Chevette.

Then I met the frat guys, who worried about their hair, their face and their clothes. Not a single one would have known what to do in the event of a flat tire. Their hands were callous-free. I remember hearing one say he was cold. In 18 years I'd never heard a man say he was cold. They seemed to complain about everything.

Even worse, despite their brooding and complaining, the girls gravitated toward them. It was crazy that a guy with a problem would be gold to a woman; yet someone who bears down when times get tough, who doesn't speak unless he can improve the silence, would actually be a turn-off.

I liken it to poker. Great poker players don't get too up or too down when they win or lose a pot. They look at poker as just being one long hand. This is how Man Code men look at romance: It's better to conserve emotion for only the most meaningful circumstances. If a few things don't get said that should, that's fine. Your job is to be the rock.

Meanwhile, women grind and focus on one hand. They must win this hand right now, because what will it say about them if they don't win? Time is running out. Non-Man Code men play into this. They emote. They reveal their innermost secrets from the jump. They present a problem the woman can solve. Even though they're bad boys, in that moment they are uncomplicated, and that satisfies the need for immediate gratification.

I saw the same thing when I went on "The Bachelorette" and shared a living space with 30 guys. The Man Code men—those who'd been around other guys their entire lives and were principally against lying about their emotions just to satisfy television's need for speed—stood absolutely no chance. The conservation of emotion is just not telegenic.

Meanwhile, the Jake Pavelka's of the world, who will fall in love and cry on cue, were willing to trade their dignity for the girl. This is why engagements from "The Bachelorette" never work. The good guys are sent packing in favor of the men who give away the plot, so to speak, in the first five minutes. When the Bachelorette and her man go home to the real world, and all of the emotion of a 10-year-relationship has been processed and distilled for a 10-episode run, where does a couple have to go from there?

Needless to say, years of losing to men who didn't know how to act around other men or how to treat women properly began to rub me the wrong way. My dad and I began talking about Man Code again, just as we had when I was younger. Every time we saw a guy not hold a door open, we'd say, "That's a Man Code violation right there."

That brings us to here, with me acknowledging that of all the career paths open to former reality stars, becoming a writer of books that pine for a bygone era of chivalry is not the most obvious to follow. But I feel a lot can be gained by my explaining the inner workings of alpha males to the fairer sex.

And as I mentioned previously, this is also a chance to right a wrong. I was not chivalrous when I appeared on "The Bachelorette," which was also when I brought the term "Man Code" to prominence. I'd be a hypocrite if I didn't acknowledge that. I think my appearance on "Bachelor Pad" helped restore the Man Code as something meaningful, and this book will complete the job.

There's a recent book out by former Disney CEO Michael Eisner called "Working Together." He talks about an ambitious study that attempted to track the origins of happiness in humans over a lifetime. The No. 1 common denominator among those who said they'd had a happy life was that they'd had some form of partner with whom they'd shared it.

It might be foolish, but I think this book might do something to help build these partnerships. By demystifying Man Code, I think I can teach you to take a straighter line to your man's heart—a straighter line than even McDonalds and a cinnamon roll can provide.

WHAT IS A MAN CODE MAN?
(AND WHY ARE WE
SO DIFFICULT?)

Much of what's to follow in this book suggests that having a Man Code Man in your life is actually desirable, and then I outline what it is we're looking for in a partner.

So it's imperative that I make this blanket statement: we Man Code men can be an absolute pain in the rear. While I think our adherence to a time-honored code keeps us grounded and ultimately makes us valuable, we are not without our head-slapping moments.

I'll use this analogy a couple times in the book: Love with a Man Code man is like a cat that brings a dead bird to its owner's doorstep to show its affection. That ain't pretty on the surface, but the underlying meaning is something very nice. We all have to learn to accept love as it's offered, not how we want it to be offered. We want happiness and partnership as much as women do; we just often go after it like a blunt instrument.

We often do not know how to show what it is we're feeling. We grow up sharpening our characters against other men, so the language of love might as well be ancient Greek to us. Even though we know it's best to just let go, it's hard to really do so and allow ourselves to be in a vulnerable position. All of our preceding life education runs completely counter to this. For being tough guys, we're a little scared.

We may never give you the quantity of affection you desire, but we'll make up for it in quality. Once we think you understand this, the ruffian surface will come crumbling down. This understanding—or lack thereof—has been the pivot point in a lot of relationships. A little of this understanding might have gone a long way for my own parents, and I suppose I want for others the happiness they couldn't have. To me, understanding equals happiness. Though I'm not married, I have had meaningful relationships of nine and four years. I've also had very middling relationships and others that were over before they started. I haven't found the perfect person, but I think that at this point—especially given the accelerated track the past two years have put me on—I understand what success and failure look like when it comes to love.

I wouldn't be surprised if the Man Code ends up being something very different from what you think. It is not the rules for an exclusive guy's guy club. It is not a rulebook that gives me a reason to push out someone who doesn't intuitively think what I do.

The Man Code is inclusive. It's about respect, integrity, accountability and pride. It's about the dirt under your fingernails and on the road beneath your feet, both literally and metaphorically. Anyone can be Man Code, whether blue collar, white collar, straight, gay, single or married. A Man Code man can exist anywhere, anytime. It's about having a basis for what you do, day in and day out. If you're a guy who gets it, no explanation is necessary. If not, no explanation is possible.

Most of it is learned and not taught. It's about subtle things, like sleeping on the side of the bed closest to the door, which is a rule I was never told but I saw in practice and felt. My dad's side of the bed was always nearest the door. It made his wife feel safe. That discrete sign of protection let all of us know that if something came through the door, he'd be standing in it to block the way. A Man Code man knows that his kids won't remember a lot of what he taught them, but they will remember how we loved their mother. (This is at the root of why many components of the Code are being lost, as dads are often not in the home anymore. More on that in the following chapter.)

Not all Man Code men like cars, watch football or watch "Old School" weekly. We're as different in our interests as women are. But Man Code men all have passion, they all know the world doesn't exist to make them happy, and they all would rather laugh than sulk.

While we might rebel against the establishment, we enjoy the order of codes. This is true of government, society and manhood. The Man Code cannot be broken, and if it is forsaken, it takes us a long time to recover our faith. Codes exist for a reason. They give us stability and order. There is the law of gravity, the rule of thumb and the code of silence, all of which are respected even if they're not understood. Be it in the boardroom, barroom or bedroom, the Code has to be obeyed at all times. It's not flexible.

As the Man Code is passed down from generation to generation, you'll find on page 24 the things I'd tell my son if he asked me how he could go about living up to the Man Code.

Now, just because we're simple doesn't mean we're easy. Why are we so damn tough to live with?

First and foremost, our method of socializing is totally the inverse of women's. We get our validation through groups. We're pack animals. But despite living our lives in public, we are astonishingly private. Women spend time in smaller groups and make their inner-worlds far better known. When these worlds collide, women have the advantage because they have a lot of experience with one-on-one. But Man Code men are baffled. When very little is personal or private, you don't really know how good that can be. It has to take us by surprise sometimes. Beyond birth and death, the most significant things in life are experienced with your partner. But nothing in our prior lives has readied us for that. To this point, everything we've done is based on conservation of emotion.

Our whole ethic is based on doing. Our whole value lies in what we do, what we produce. We are about forward motion. Women simply require our presence, and this is also very perplexing.

LESSONS TO TEACH A BUDDING MAN CODE MAN

Always care. Take pride in your country and your community.

If something needs getting done, do it. Stop thinking that what you do doesn't make a difference.

Take responsibility. Look another man in the eye and take responsibility for your actions.

Learn your lessons.

Make sure you pass the vouch test. If someone had to speak to your character, could they do it without reservation?

Let another man shine. Always make another man look like a hero in front of his son.

Gain perspective. Do all you can to understand the world, so you can have perspective on your successes and your failures.

Treat each play like it's your last. Literally and metaphorically.

Stand out. But do it without standing out.

Know who you are, and who you ain't.

Be a stand-up guy. Know that at some point in your life you'll have nothing to stand on but your reputation.

Have passion.

Be honest. Always.

On the job, Man Code is the real CEO. While it may be tempting to do an end-around on your colleague, you don't do it if it's at his expense. Be a friend on the job as much as you are off it.

Have something to say. No opinion means no brains.

Want it. You have to want to succeed like you want to breathe.

No matter your success, you need to wake up each day with an underdog mentality.

Love the one you're with.

You are what you do. Not what you say you'll do.

We are stubborn not just with you, but with other men, as well. The only difference is that when we clash with other guys, we meet force with force. Women are left to deal with the aftermath of this. Every day, at the end of every negotiation or confrontation, we're left with the feeling of having won or lost. We bring home a lot of baggage.

The best compliment we can give women—who are so nurturing—is to let you help us. But it wounds our pride to ask not just for your help, but anyone's.

Finally, the thing about being in a committed relationship or marriage is that it doesn't negotiate. You have to give up being the king a little bit. Things are taken out of your hands. Before we become husbands or fathers, we can be a little self-obsessed. Eventually we learn that's what it's all about: the delight of being a servant. Laurence Olivier said that the greatest thing you could aspire to in life is to be a good servant. This sounds ridiculous until you've lived it. I'm not sure the true joy of being a servant to someone else really reveals itself to us until later in life, when you look at your kids and realize you wouldn't have had it any other way. Women spend their whole lives getting ready for that moment. They yearn for it. Men have to come to the realization they want it.

Fortunately, Man Code men tend to be as specific in our weaknesses as in our strengths. And like women, those things that are our strengths can also be our weaknesses. It's like the Greek concept of *hamartia*: your greatest flaw is often your greatest strength. By understanding Man Code, my hope is this will give you insight into our flaws and strengths, all at once.

WHERE HAVE ALL
THE MAN CODE MEN GONE?

Women often ask, "Where have all the good men gone?"
To which I say: I'm with you, sisters.

There might come a day when I'm less recognized than I am now, when fewer people will care about what I have to say. I'll confess this book is a bit of a Trojan horse. In the guise of explaining the Man Code, I also want to put my finger down on this page in history and say, "What the hell is going on out there? Where are the Man Code men going?"

As I said in the previous chapter, a Man Code man can come in any shape, size or package. But somewhere within a man—be he straight or gay, single or married, young or old—needs to lie a *man*, if you know what I mean.

Just on a superficial level, whatever happened to:

Drinking like a man? These days, too many guys drink like they're on *Sex and the City*. Whatever happened to going to the bar, ordering a stiff one, and letting it linger? I'm talking Scotch, whiskey or bourbon, with the only variable being soda and/or ice.

Hammering a nail? When the first step to fixing a faucet is getting out the Yellow Pages, we've got a problem. When I was a kid, you could be a barrister or a bartender, it didn't matter— on the weekend you were a handyman.

Men's night? If you call a "guy's night out" a "guy's night out," you're already lost. I'm talking about having a regular table at a steakhouse and throwing down. You don't ask permission to have this night out, it's understood you will have it.

Knowing how to throw a punch? We don't handle things man-to-man these days, we handle them man to blog. Even our football stars have taken to Tweeting their barbs. Throw in the litigiousness of our society, where the loser of a brawl is likely to file suit the next day, and you've got a generation of men who can't throw a punch. Worse yet, they can't take a punch or accept when they're whipped.

Icons? The cultural icons of past generations were icons for a reason. But the cultural icons today don't have anything but a hefty bank account. We still value fame, and yet almost anyone can become famous at any time, myself included. This instills two great ideals in young men: First, talent doesn't mean much; and second, hard work doesn't mean much. I'd like to think that in the past, you "knew who you knew" and "had what you had" from working the way you did.

Letting a man look you in the eye? In my dad's business, half the battle was face-to-face interaction, getting out from behind the desk and leaving the confines of the office. But guys like me are running their lives from a laptop. Socially, many of us know nothing outside our computer screen. Technology has made us lazy, unable to interact in the real world and all under the guise of convenience.

The underdog mentality? In my dad's day, you were the paperboy before you owned the paper. Now everyone just wants to be happy all the time. Television and other media has led to this self-fulfilling prophecy where we think everyone is partying all the time and everyone is hooking up three times a day.

Everyone thinks the world owes them happiness. Ironically, the world is now full of spoiled pussyfooters with no hustle. Instead of working hard to make happiness a reality, they put in half-assed work and quit when it doesn't work out. Now we're just a bunch of mercenaries.

There's a speech in "Fight Club" that I find to be a great assessment of where we are as men:

> "Advertising has us chasing cars and clothes, working jobs we hate so we can buy shit we don't need. We're the middle children of history, man. No purpose or place. We have no great war. No Great Depression. Our great war's a spiritual war...our Great Depression is our lives. We've all been raised on television to believe that one day we'd all be millionaires and movie gods and rock stars. But we won't."

Men today have lost what took centuries to become part of our DNA. We're impatient, indecisive, and distinctly un-excellent. How'd we get in this financial crisis we're in now? No one wanted to work his way up from the bottom. Sure, these softies existed in past generations, but they used to kill themselves off before they got far. Not now.

How on earth did this happen? This country was built on enterprise, guts and immigrant hustle. How'd we lose our way, with the blood of the Greatest Generation still pumping through our veins?

Divorces. Dad isn't at home for two-thirds of American children. Dads are the ones who showed us how to be in the world, and now they're gone.

Losses in manual labor. Now the blue-collar work force has moved on to jobs that don't require calluses, or those jobs have been moved overseas to less-expensive destinations.

Indoor kids. A man cuts his teeth outdoors. At family gatherings, the boys used to go outside and play ball, measuring themselves up against one another. Now the cousins all shut themselves in a back room and play video games.

The redefinition of sports. I admire the balls it takes to skateboard down a railing or take your BMX off a sick ramp. And I appreciate this has provided a destination for kids who might not otherwise be team athletes. But I think we're also losing kids who might otherwise be team players to these things, and I find that's unfortunate. I think you find out who you are within the context of a team. You win, you lose, and you find out something about yourself either way.

A recent story in *Newsweek* called "Men's Lib" supports this:

As the U.S. economy has transitioned from brawn to brain over the past three decades, a growing number of women have gone off to work. Men's share of the labor force has declined from 70 percent in 1945 to less than 50 percent today, and in the country's biggest cities, young, single, childless women—that is, the next generation—earn 8 percent more than their male peers. Women have matched or overtaken men as a percentage of students in college and graduate school, while men have retained their lead in alcoholism, suicide, homelessness, violence, and criminality. Factor in the Great Recession, which has decimated male-heavy industries like construction and manufacturing, and it's no wonder so many deadline anthropologists are down on men. But while the state of American manhood has inspired plenty of anxious trend pieces, few observers have bothered to address the obvious question: if men are going off the rails, how do they get back on track?

What bothers me about this isn't the ascension of women to their rightful place. It's that men aren't contributing their share. It's disgusting. Our failure is causing women to be everything to all people.

Worse yet, I see female friends of mine dating these simps. Women, this is evolution time. You cannot accept a man who is a non-contributor. You might feel sorry for him because of his daddy issues, his downsizing or his carpal tunnel syndrome, but you should not accept him as your spouse. If he is your spouse, he needs to buck up or face the consequences. Have him read Tom Brokaw's book *The Greatest Generation*, which is full of stories of men who fought in World War I, came home, lost everything in the Great Depression and still managed to keep their feet moving. It is impossible for a man to dignify himself while sitting on the couch.

It was once incumbent upon men to accept women as their equal. Now women need to help men get themselves back up to equal status.

THE DIFFERENCE BETWEEN A MAN CODE MAN AND A BAD BOY

When I began researching this project, I found to my great surprise a large number of existing books by men teaching women how to understand "bad boys." I found an even greater number of magazine articles—to my even greater surprise—from women's magazines offering fellow ladies tips on getting their bad boys to behave.

These books and articles essentially teach women how to land men they shouldn't want in the first place. This presumes that women have no other options, which isn't true.

Let me tell you now, a Man Code man is not a bad boy. Please don't confuse the two. There is a little naughtiness in all of us, but we save that for our buddies.

Bad Boy-ism is all about "bros before ho's," "if you don't drink this shot you're a candy ass," and the blind leading the blind. That's not Man Code; that's boy code. A bad boy is a cliché. Why would you want to be with a cliché?

Don't get me wrong: Man Code men are complex and sometimes downright pains in the ass, for all the reasons I've mentioned previously. Man Code men and bad boys might share some rugged external characteristics. But to me, bad boy-ism is just a romanticized excuse for prolonged adolescence; a euphemism for me-first behavior. We pass through bad boy-ism (when we're 12) on the way to learning the Man

Code. Forgive my language here, but to put as fine a point as possible on this, "bad boy" is code for "dick."

Underneath a bad boy is something that's broken, whereas within the Man Code man there's something very solid—almost so solid that we're scared to deviate from it. The fundamental difference between us and them is honesty, plain and simple. Given time and a great deal of patience, you'll discover that a Man Code man is something of a feminist. He's a woman's best friend. He'll stand up for her and never let her down, and wants her to be empowered so long as he can be, too. He will reassure her when she feels insecure and comfort her when she's questioning herself. He'll inspire her to do things she never thought she could; to live without fear and forget regret.

The Man Code is a standard. Bad boy-ism is the low bar. Ulterior motives are entirely a bad boy thing. A Man Code man absolutely has red-blooded carnal desires. But he manages to have them while also being on the woman's side.

Conversely, to a bad boy, women are conquests who will live on as nothing more than supporting characters in buffoonish stories. A Man Code man is ultimately looking for a great romance, so long as it melds with the continuity and positive predictability he requires to feel comfortable. We might seem like players, but that's only because no one has intrigued us enough or had patience enough with us to let one another's substance shine through.

I generally find that Man Code men are serial monogamists. Now, not every relationship is as important as the last, but he doesn't have several of them going on in parallel. I've had two long-term in my life, the first of which lasted nine years spanning from junior high to college. The other relationship, also with a truly great woman, lasted four years. I remain close friends with both and am friends with the partners they have today. The quality that most defines a Man Code Man is loyalty, and it's what he most values in his friends, be they buddies or romantic attachments.

David Good

WHY YOU WANT
A MAN CODE MAN

The Man Code is good for women, though I know it might not always appear that way. Stubborn, reserved, overly loyal, so hell-bent on making things simple that we make them complicated—what's not to love, right? But it's true.

If for no other reason, the Man Code is good for women because it serves as a tether. It ties us to the dirt road. Most importantly, it brings us back to center when we've behaved in a non-Man Code way. There's nothing worse to a Man Code man than deviating from the code, and he'll know it before anyone else will. You won't need to tell him.

In the film "A Few Good Men," Jack Nicholson's character said, "You want me on that wall. You need me on that wall." I think women need Man Code men, they just might not know it.

In other words—and pardon me for my language here—it's an absolute truth in life that if you don't have someone (or something) calling you on your shit, you're lost. As I said, the irony of my announcing "Man Code" to the world is that when I did it, I was behaving in a way that was a little scary, and certainly didn't make it seem like the Code was anyone's friend. Part of the reason I'm writing this at all is because it did a disservice to the Code as well as my father and the others who taught it to me.

My actual experience when I went on "The Bachelorette" was a good one. I met some great guys, had a good time, and any minor annoyances about guys in the house were just that: minor. I won the first-impression rose, was picked to play with the Harlem Globetrotters ... once in a lifetime experiences. I'm a comical guy, and I was cutting up Jillian Harris, our Bachelorette, and the other guys. I was upbeat and outgoing.

But within the context of the month I spent in the house, I gave producers some material that would haunt me in the end. When I first saw how my actions were positioned on the show—stretched to a three-episode ordeal that I felt was not indicative of their context within the house—I was angry. I blamed the producers for drawing me out and then giving me what I felt was a "bad edit." I blamed the guys at whom my anger was directed, Jake Pavelka and Juan Barbieri. Initially I was indignant about my actions but embarrassed about my language. I was angry at the show for making a mockery of me and the Code.

Soon, though, I knew that behavior would be my legacy if I didn't accept all the responsibility. This was the Code calling me home. The show exposed my flaws. Sure enough, "Bachelor Pad" came around the corner, allowing me to set the record straight.

The reality of making a reality show is that you are sequestered in a house with 30 guys with no phones, computers, televisions or other means of distraction. You're like a jury in a capital case. You are given a fair bit of top-shelf alcohol, though, which loosens the mechanism and let's the mouth run free. Pretty soon, you're bored, you're impatient, you've seen the girl for 15 minutes over five days, and your competitive juices get flowing.

Keep in mind, I come from the Midwest, where even metrosexuals drive pickup trucks and wear Wranglers. My exposure to guys who were camera-conscious, thought endlessly about how they appeared, and cried at the drop of a hat were limited. And by "limited," I mean I'd had more exposure to people from Venus.

But now I'm in a house with guys who change their shirts every time a camera is around, and who don't know how to so much as turn on a gas grille. Most of the guys were acting like guys, giving each other a hard time and kidding around, but a couple of them couldn't take it, which seemed insane to me. I mean, that's how we show we like one another. Worse yet, they're getting more time with the girl than I am. I feel like I'm losing and I can't believe it.

On one occasion, the cameras came around and Juan and Jake ran inside to change their clothes. Most of the guys are in scrubs and stupid clothes like shorts and bandanas, acting like we're living in the wilderness, and these guys are in argyle vests and Polo shirts with designer jeans. On another occasion, we were playing beer pong and doing shots, and Juan faked as though he'd taken his, as we saw him throw it in the bushes. Minor infractions, I know, but in that concentrated environment there's nothing to do but scrutinize behavior. The show's producers are expert at creating that cauldron, as they should be. You are constantly in the waiting room, making waiting room conversation. Nothing real is at stake, but you start to feel like there is.

Growing up, I was taught that a man has to defend the pack. When there's something to be said, you say it. I want to be the guy in that doorway not letting the fakers get past.

So one night we're doing what we're always doing, and I'm outside talking with one of the guys about Juan's behavior that day. Juan came outside and said, "What are you guys talking about?" and I said, "You. You broke Man Code." That would have been fine, but then the blood starts going, the booze starts kicking in, and I'm acting scary, all for the consumption of 15 million people. I lost control of the conversation and my actions, and inadvertently made great television. I could say that we're all products of our environment, and my environment had been truckers, not bankers, and I had a filthy mouth and overly direct demeanor. I'm a Merle Haggard, Bobby Knight guy. I don't put lotion on my hands and I don't wear pink shirts. But we all have to transcend our environment at some point for one reason or another. Then I wasn't particularly chivalrous toward our Bachelorette, and the spiral continued. Again, that moment felt very out of context on TV, as we were laughing before and after it, but still, I should have been wise to the fact that this show wasn't going to run unedited. The producers aren't there to serve our story, they're there to serve the audience and its desire to be entertained.

When the show aired, I went to my family and friends and apologized. They weren't terribly upset, but I owed them that.

When I was asked to go back on "Bachelor Pad," they obviously thought I'd make the same contribution. Seeing Juan was also in the house, this was all the more clear. But going into that program, I'd reconciled my past behavior and wanted to do better. This time I was going to help, not harm. What I should have said to Juan was, "Listen, man. The guys are talking about you. You're putting a lot of pressure on yourself. Just relax and come hang out." Help, not harm. Redemption. Accountability. That's Man Code. I'd had a chance to watch myself on TV and see how I really act. Not everyone gets that chance, to pinpoint the things you really need to improve. Given a second chance, I wanted to represent myself, my family and the Code better, and that's what I think I did.

To me, this call to accountability is Man Code. The Man Code didn't drive me to misbehave; it drove me to make it right. From a woman's perspective, there are a lot worse things than having a man that's beholden to something bigger than him, who doesn't play games when it comes to the truth. There are worse things than a guy who has a strong sense of right and wrong, and who defies trends for something that is time-honored tradition.

These days, with my win on "Bachelor Pad" in my recent past, it's a struggle to stay on track. I've been thrown a lot of notoriety and social power. People approach me for the wrong reasons, and I have the potential to approach them for the wrong reasons, too. It's a true test. I feel fortunate to have the Man Code to guide me.

HOW CAN YOU TELL IF HE'S A MAN CODE MAN?

There are certain types that can be pegged just by looking at them. Bad boys, metrosexuals...You can spot them from a mile away. This isn't the case with Man Code men, given that we come in a variety of packages.

More than looks, the essence of a Man Code man is in the intangibles. At a bar, he buys the first round, and treats waitresses and bartenders like he would his doctor or lawyer. When he's walking down the sidewalk with his lady, he stays on the side closest to the street, all the better positioned to deflect the unexpected. When he's out with his mom, he buttons up a bit, edits out the rough humor, and stands a little straighter. At work, he's the first in and the last to leave.

Much as your man's buddies can initially seem like a thorn in your side, his role within that group can tell you a lot about the sort of person he is and the type of future you're bound to have with him. First and foremost, does he have good friends? Do his friends come to him when they have trouble? Does he share information that was told to him in private? When his buddy asks him a question, does your man give him an honest answer? Is he the sort of guy who'll tease his buddy a little bit, but if an outsider gives that friend a hard time, your man will kick his ass?

Another gauge of a Man Code man is what I call "first-world problems vs. third-world problems." In other words, are his problems ones that would be considered problems anywhere in the world and not just in his privileged universe? A Man Code man will be concerned with health, family and the ability to improve the lot in life of those most important to him. A non-Man Code man will worry about his looks, his car, his house and his social standing—things that would not be of concern to someone trying to survive from one day to the next.

Is your guy a Man Code man? This quiz might bear that out.

THE MAN CODE QUIZ

Where does your man sleep?
☐ All over the bed
☒ Closest to the door
☐ Furthest from the door

Does your man open the door for you?
☐ Never
☒ Always
☐ Only on special occasions

On the first date did your man pay for dinner?
☒ Yes
☐ No

Does your man treat with respect that one friend you have who he doesn't particularly relate to?
☒ Yes
☐ No

Does your man take pride in his name and how people view him?
☒ Yes
☐ No

How long does your man take to get ready to go out?
☑ Under 30 minutes
☐ Between 30 minutes and one hour
☐ Over an hour

Does your man change the way he treats you in front of his friends?
☐ Yes
☐ No

When it comes to work, is your man the first in and the last to leave?
☐ Yes
☐ No

Does your man have a best friend? Old friends?
☑ Yes
☐ No

Whether you agree with them or not, does he seem to have a core set of beliefs?
☑ Yes
☐ No

Does your man make jokes at the expense of others?
☐ Yes
☑ No

Does your man give up his seat to you or others?
☑ Yes
☐ No

When you're lost, does he take charge and look for a map, or does he wait for someone else to figure it out?
☐ Takes charge
☐ Waits for others

Do people call on your man when they need help? Is he the sort of guy who others could call in the middle of the night and he'll come get them?

☒ Yes

☐ No

Does your man try whenever possible to do things for himself before calling someone to do it for him?

☒ Yes

☐ No

Does your man worry about the material possessions he has or doesn't have?

☐ Yes

☒ No

If applicable, does your man talk too much or too little?

☐ Too much

☒ Too little

If anything, does your man have too much or too little pride?

☐ Too much

☐ Too little

Does your man treat his mother respectfully?

☐ Yes

☐ No

Does your man blame his problems on others, or does he take responsibility for his actions?

☐ Blames on others

☐ Takes responsibility

Does your man have his own ideas, or do his ideas sound like ones you've heard before?
☐ His own ideas
☐ Ones you've heard before

Would you attribute whatever success your man has had to hard work or luck?
☐ Hard work
☐ Luck

If anything, does your man spend too much or save too much?
☐ Spends too much
☑ Saves too much

ANSWERS:
1 – b, 2 – b, 3 – a, 4 – a, 5 – a, 6 – a, 7 – a, 8 – b, 9 – a, 10 – a, 11 – a, 12 – b, 13 – a, 14 – a, 15 – a, 16 – a, 17 – a, 18 – b, 19 – a, 20 – a, 21 – b, 22 – a, 23 – a, 24 – b, 25 – a.

As far as I'm concerned, your man needs to score 25 for 25 to be considered a Man Code man. The common denominator among all of these is that protector gene I mentioned earlier. Every strength and fault of a Man Code man is derived from that gene, as his default is to protect. In the worst-case scenario, he's protecting himself. But in the best cases, he's protecting you, his family and his friends in some way, shape or form.

WHAT A MAN CODE MAN IS NOT

Michelangelo was once asked about his process in making "David." He answered, "I just cut away everything that did not look like my statue, and soon it stood there before me."

Far be it from me to compare the Man Code to a work of art, but there is one apt comparison: In explaining the code, it's sometimes simpler to explain what it is not as it is to explain what it is.

You can say this about Man Code followers: at least we know who we ain't.

Much as the Man Code was a theme for me throughout my life, it didn't truly crystallize for me until I became involved in the process surrounding "The Bachelorette" and then "Bachelor Pad."

When I first became acquainted with these programs, I was being considered to be "The Bachelor." I was "discovered" in a bar in Tampa, and was of course flattered and enthusiastic about the prospect of being chosen. (The spot ultimately went to Jason Mesnick.)

Entertaining as they are, for a Bachelor to be telegenic, he has to behave in a way that is fundamentally different from anything I've been exposed to. You need to emote, profess being in love with the idea of love, and be willing to make a woman your life all the while simultaneously weighing your options with other women on the side. In other words, it's all a little insincere, and to me it's not surprising that not many of those relationships last too far beyond the day the show goes dark.

When the roles were reversed on "The Bachelorette," I found myself in an amplified reality. There are a bunch of bulls in a pen with one female. Competitive instincts take over. Sure you can win the girl. But to me the real question was, amidst all of this jockeying for position, could you still win respect and friendship with your fellow guys?

Again, I confess that I behaved badly on "The Bachelorette." But I did manage to win the first impression rose and be chosen by the Harlem Globetrotters to be their teammate for the day. I also emerged from the show with the friendship of the majority of my housemates. I did some things wrong, but in an intense atmosphere, I did some things right, too.

My castmate, Jake Pavelka, was in love with love, and willing to say and do anything to find it. It was not surprising to any of us that he was chosen to the next Bachelor; nor was it surprising that his relationship with Vienna crashed so spectacularly. When all the emotions are revealed up front and no mystery is retained, the relationship just deflates. This leads to frustration, which leads to anger, which leads to screaming on national television in a fashion that tears down all good will you've spent more than a year building. Very non-productive, very self-destructive, and very non-Man Code, because you've not only lost the trust of your fellow men in the house and in the audience, but you've also alienated women, as well. When you're not true to a code, it's impossible to be true to anyone at all.

So far as I'm concerned, a Man Code man wants love to happen when it happens. He doesn't search for it like a recruiter trying to fill a position. Man Code men don't feel lost without a partner; nor should a woman. We're looking for a friend, and we hope you are, too. If that develops in front of 10 cameras and 15 million people, God bless. It's just not likely.

The Internet is littered with bullet-pointed lists of Man Rule Do's and Don'ts. "Never share an umbrella with another man." "Never date the sister of a guy you've known for more than 24 hours." "Never complain about a free drink." "On a road trip, the strongest bladder determines pit stops, not the weakest."

This is not that list. Instead, my goal is to show you what a Man Code man is by showing you what he is not.

The following might also be called "Advice We'd Give Our Sisters," as in, "Sister, never trust a man who..."

Why are these axioms on pages 52–53 true? Experience tells me they are. The Man Code is unspoken; if a guy needs it spelled out for him, there's your answer.

HE'S NOT A MAN CODE MAN IF HE...

- reminds you more of a cat than a dog. In fact, never trust a man who could own a dog but chooses to own a cat instead. And for that matter, never trust a single man who owns a dog smaller than a typical cat.

- posts a Facebook status update with anything that isn't funny and/or self-deprecating.

- doesn't like sports, particularly the strain of man who pretends to like sports but doesn't really.

- splits the dinner bill according to who ate what. (Along those same lines, never trust a man who will even consider splitting the bill with you. A Man Code man pays the freight, or wants to, even on his birthday.)

- fails to give away his seat on a subway or bus to everyone except other men of his same age and stature.

- tells you what you should and shouldn't eat.

- uses the words "cute" or "classy."

- can't tell a story. (There's a big difference between a storyteller and a motormouth, which is a guy who thinks out loud and constantly seeks approval.)

- drinks anything pink or red.

- would rather stay in a hotel than on his buddy's couch.

- seems incapable or raising a son who becomes a man better than himself.

- complains about how much things cost when he takes you out.

- is not a good tipper.

- comparison shops for anything besides cars and houses.

- has a mustache that was not grown for an ironic purpose.

- has a haircut that looks like he could be in Congress.

- tells you within five minutes of meeting you where he went to college, how much money he makes or the car he drives.

- asks for credit for things he should do; i.e., raising his children, working hard, being faithful to his wife, etc.

- has a garage full of new tools.

- gets to work at 9 a.m. or leaves punctually at 5.

- roots for a team that is not from his hometown, and that team has won a championship within the last three years.

- compensates for his lack of actual intelligence, insight or humor by simply speaking louder.

- talks about past girlfriends or, even worse, sexual conquests. (A good rule of thumb is that the number of girls a guy brags about being with is inverse to the number he's actually been with.)

THINGS WOMEN MUST ACCEPT
ABOUT MAN CODE MEN

The Code is the code. Men cling to it like the building inspector. While it is the duty of a man to compromise on some things if he wants his romantic relationship to work, there are certain things that are immutable, intractable, irreversible, chiseled in stone and written in ink.

The Man Code may as well be in our DNA. To ask us to change it would be akin to asking a fish to ride a bicycle.

To a certain extent, you must accept our love as it's given. We are the cat that brings a dead bird to the doorstep of its master as a sign of affection. It may not be pretty, but it's love nonetheless.

The first thing you cannot change is our loyalty to our friends. More than anything, Man Code men prize loyalty. We are pack animals; a band of brothers. The great thing I have in my life is all these friends who are family to me, and it's been that way for 20 years. They keep me on the straight and narrow, and I do the same for them. We have our own lives and families. But we have our rituals: golf on the weekends, games on Sundays. We work hard and play hard. If a man truly follows the code, he won't put you behind these guys, but you will sometimes feel as if you're standing shoulder to shoulder with them, and that isn't always pleasant. But the second you try to separate us from them, we'll start to separate ourselves from you.

Man Code men and women differ fundamentally on love. When men are officially in a romantic relationship with a lady, you take us straight to the front of the line, which feels great. But for men, love is a meritocracy. When we begin dating you, you queue up with the other friends and work your way up to the front gradually by winning our trust. That's not to say that you are unimportant. You are VERY important. But we tend to treat all our significant friends as very important. We can expand infinitely, yet the individual relationships remain precious, and none more than the one we have with our lady over time. Unfortunately, there's no replacement for time but more time.

We spend our whole lives finding ourselves in groups. That's why guys fantasize about being Army men. It's not the activity; it's the camaraderie. It's the sense of belonging; a second family. Whenever an athlete retires and he's asked what he misses, he always says it's the locker room; the traveling with 25 guys.

Women are more intimate. They get their energy from one-on-one time, which is awesome. It's just not our way. You often hear guys say, "I love that guy like a brother." You don't often hear women say, "I love her like a sister." Men say this because our relationships aren't subtle. You're my family. You've been loyal to me, I'll be loyal to you. It's something we start learning at an early age. As John Lennon said, "You have to understand the little boy inside the man..."

To this end, I can tell you that a woman who has created a second family much like a man would is extremely attractive. On the flipside, ladies, if your man struggles with fitting into that group dynamic among other men, he's not Man Code.

When I walked onto the set of "Bachelor Pad," a show where we'd ultimately eliminate one another, I could've told you exactly who were going to last among the guys: Kiptyn Locke, Jesse Kovacs and Jesse Beck. Why? It wasn't because we were all friends coming into it and had an unwritten contract. These guys were all Man Code. The others had a much harder time weaving themselves into the guy fabric. I knew it within 30 seconds. Regardless of what made sense from a strategic standpoint, I knew loyalty would be rewarded even if it defied logic. That's exactly what happened. When he was interviewed, Kovacs said, "Dave and I had one plan going into this: To have no plan. Mission accomplished." Despite this fact, we lasted to the end. The Code is the code, wherever you go. We might make bad Bachelors, but we strong, silent types are good for other things!

Loyalty is loyalty, and it doesn't end. If a guy does me a solid at any point, I will drive across country to fix his flat tire 10 years later. Women think this is crazy, and it probably is. But it's as inevitable as gravity. The greater the pressure, the fiercer the loyalty becomes. We want to be Butch and Sundance, living or dying together. Our fantasy is not to die in our wife's arms, but to go out in a blaze of glory.

What you need to understand is that this is a good thing. In Malcolm Gladwell's *Outliers*, he said that to be considered an expert at something, you need to have 10,000 hours in the saddle. Well, Man Code men have gotten the repetitions necessary to know what true faithfulness and friendship mean. Non-Man Code men likely have not. To them, fidelity is just a nice idea.

Another thing women must accept is that while we run in packs and are loyal to the end, Man Code men still keep a lot of things private. We might be friends with a couple who are having a hard time. You and the woman can go out and get down to what's happening in their marriage before the coffee is served. Meanwhile, I can go out golfing with the guy and come back seven hours later with no new information. Why? Because if he wanted to talk about it, he would have. At least that's the way Man Code men look at it. Plus, there was golf to be played and why let feelings get in the way of a good time?

That might sound crass, but it's true. Intimate conversation is sport to women. That is not the case for men. Sport is sport to men. Talks about feelings are few and far between. This is the 10,000 hours model flipped on its head. When it comes to talking about feelings and being introspective, you are at least 10,000 hours ahead of us, and that margin grows all the time. We have no practice at it, so you can't expect us to be good at it right away. Give us time and we'll get there. Just accept that nothing leading up to our relationship with you has readied us for what we're about to experience.

Just as a woman with friends is attractive, so is a woman with secrets. With Facebook, Twitter, et al, we live in a world where public is the new private. This is one huge turnoff to Man Code men. Discretion is sexy to a man, and it is a rarer commodity all the time, it seems. Holding a little something back will go a long way. I don't think men are built to know everything all at once, and we're certainly not built to reveal everything at once. Love is highly uncertain, and it goes against our protective instincts to leave ourselves defenseless.

Women just get there much, much faster. They take chances on love, and Man Code men are far more cautious, both because we're uncertain about these feelings and because we're protecting ourselves and you. Our pragmatism is for our benefit and yours.

Women give in to the supernatural far more easily, be it in the form of love, spiritual faith, or other. Man Code men are less certain about those things. This might not be a good thing—who couldn't use a little more faith and love, right? But again, it's in our DNA. You can't fight it.

Women must also accept that men are competitive. We look for it. Iron sharpens iron, and men sharpen men. If your man is scared to compete, and therefore scared to lose, get ready for life in the middle of the road. Who wants that? I can tell you right now that I will race my grandmother to the grocery store. My observation is that women don't always like our competitive natures, but they do like successful men, and this is a juxtaposition they need to come to terms with.

What goes into competing is deserving to win, and that means hard work. I was at the high school gym at 5:30 a.m. every, single morning for four years. I wanted to shoot a thousand jumpers before my competition was out of bed, and I still look at life the same way. I have lost in sports, business and relationships, and it was like poison.

If you're with a Man Code man now and you're in your 20s or older, chances are your man has had a relationship before you and somewhere along the line it went badly. This feels like a loss. Sometimes it's hard to get back in the game. If the other team's center has been swatting away shot after shot, eventually you're going to stop shooting for a while. We have to get the indication that this is a game we can win.

Part of our competitive nature is that we are chasing our fathers, and that is something women have to accept. If the dad in question was absent, we're chasing down his ghost. If we has present, we're chasing down his example. One of the worst feelings I could imagine having would be that of falling short of my dad's example, which was gigantic.

My dad didn't have two nickels to rub together, but somehow financed a semi-truck, which over the years he turned into a $7 million a year business. I felt a need to show him, God and everybody that I was cut from the same cloth. Right out of college I got a little apartment in Cincinnati and went to work for a shipping brokerage. Six days a week (and often seven), I was the first in and last to leave. They eventually liked my work so much that they moved me to a new office in Tampa, which given my small-town roots felt like going to the moon.

Man Code men are not driven by money. The money is merely symbolic of something else. I remember one point when my dad could have gotten more money for selling his business out than doing what he was doing. An old guy we called One-Eyed John said to me, "I guarantee you he won't do it," and he didn't. That struck a chord with me. Someone once wrote, "We are all our fathers' shadows writ small." We're out there trying to prove we can throw our own shadows.

You also have to understand that a man dignifies himself by working. If you're with a man who seems perfectly content not working, run. Run for the hills, because that is not a dignified man. That is why, should we lose our jobs, we are beyond devastated. It will supercede all other emotion. It gets back to our protective and competitive natures. If we're not working, by all standards we're failing.

In concluding this chapter, I'll get back to my earlier example of the cat bringing the bird to the doorstep. Once women understand that men show their affection in a variety of ways, they'll be much happier. Sometimes we're saying "I love you" loud and clear, with actions instead of words. When we work hard, when we're saving our money, when we're simply spending time with you—all of that represents a huge compliment if you're willing to see it.

Women care about the medium as much as the message, and they shouldn't. When a man says thank you, let him do it any way he can. Keep your eyes and heart open.

We are economical with our words, and that can be frustrating. But as with anything rare, it's more valuable when you find it. We resist paying you the compliment of saying that we need your help. But when we do, it means a lot.

If you need a Greek chorus of men praising and loving you day and night, you will not find love with a Man Code man, plain and simple. To us, that doesn't feel like authentic friendship, and friendship is how you move to the front of the line.

David Good

WHAT MAN CODE MEN VALUE

Guys love that scene in the movie "Reservoir Dogs" where Mr. White, Mr. Orange, Mr. Blonde, Mr. Pink and Nice Guy Eddie are walking toward the camera, all in their black suits and black ties, heading off to do their last job. Why? Because even though they're off to do a bad deed, they're a band of brothers. That's why at our weddings, Man Code men all try to recreate that shot with our groomsmen. That shot appears in movies from "The Magnificent Seven" to "Tombstone," and I'm a sucker for every one.

I've said over and over that loyalty is currency for Man Code men. What we value is being needed. To us there is no greater compliment. We are raised to one day be needed, and one of the great things my parents did for me was allow me to be needed at an early age. Seven year olds can't even tie their shoes, and yet I was doing serious work on our farm by that age. They didn't do this to get some easy labor out of me. Knowing the Code, my dad knew this was the best way to compliment me. By letting me be needed, he was saying he was proud of me and who I was becoming.

Man Code men raise their sons to be needed, to be ready when that compliment is given, be it by his friends, his spouse, his kids or his teammates.

Needing to be needed is why I fantasized from an early age about being in the military. I loved that you could have no bad days in the military. You cannot be the weak link. From the moment you wake to the moment you sleep, you're needed.

I ultimately went to college to play sports, which led to a career, and the military life eluded me. But it's still an ethic I subscribe to. I have a tattoo on my arm that's commonly found in the military. It has the slogan "Death Before Dishonor" written in a coiling scroll wrapped around a dagger. The saying was used by military units at least as early as ancient Rome. It relates to the code of silence, and it means that I'll die before I violate your trust. It's not just an American code, either. For example, it was advocated in the Japanese bushido code of samurai warriors who would rather die than live with the dishonor brought on by surrender. Even as late as the 1970s, Japanese soldiers of World War II were still being discovered on Pacific islands where word of the end of the war had never reached them.

Women tend to not understand the need to be needed in this way and sometimes they think it's foolish. When I was in college, a buddy came to visit me who'd had a scrape with the law earlier. One more and he'd be in serious trouble. We were out late one night drinking beers like college kids do, and we stumbled out of a house with open containers. Sure enough, a couple police cars come by and slam on their brakes. We started running, and the cop was right behind my buddy. I had two behind me, then veered in front of the one behind him, and eventually got all the cops chasing me alone while the others got away. My mother was furious, but down deep I think she understood.

I have countless stories of brawls I've jumped into that I didn't need to, and other stories of buddies jumping in to save me at their own peril.

The truth is, at those times when I jumped in, I did it as much for myself as I did for them. I wanted to be needed. It lets me know I'm OK in the world. I want people to know that when the time comes I'll stand and deliver; that I'll keep showing up. Man Code men tend to be old-school guys who are throwbacks to an America that never lost a war or ran a deficit, and being a man was a lot clearer of a proposition. I hear about guys like San Francisco Mayor Gavin Newsom, who bedded his best friend/campaign chairman's wife, or San Antonio Spurs point guard Tony Parker, whose marriage finally ended when he was caught texting with his teammates' wife, and I feel like we are really losing our way. These are our leaders; our role models?

I think to my eulogy. What do I want people to say about me? I want them to say that I was never less than a perfect friend and that I kept showing up. That I took the dirt road in all things. That there were certain things in life I knew were absolute.

As the women in our lives, we need you to encourage us to be needed, allow us to be needed, and make us feel as though we are. Man Code men look forward to the chance to defend your honor and show you they are there for you and will do anything to make you feel safe.

STUMBLING BLOCKS ON
THE WAY TO LOVE

The purpose of writing this chapter is not to poke fun at or criticize women for all the ways they manage to take romance off the tracks with Man Code men. We are just as often the culprits.

But it bears mentioning that there are a few common denominators that I've experienced with women, and these have been repeated to me as having been experienced by other Man Code men.

Wanting to change us. The late actor Tony Curtis used to repeat this lymric a lot when asked about relationships: "You cannot ask a fish not to swim. It's the only thing that makes him him." In other words, "It's confusing to say that you love me but you also want to change me."

In my opinion, the biggest fundamental mistakes made in dating are these: Women get involved with men thinking they can change them; and men get involved with women thinking they'll never change. So while we're baffled that you could be anything other than the fun college girl we met when you were 21, you're frustrated that you can't surgically take the Man Code out of the man.

You cannot change a man, which is why you want one who lives by a code. I might choose myself to make a change if I feel the consequences of the change outweigh the benefits. But I won't change something that is fundamental to who I am no matter how much I love you, and I'll resent you for asking. I get it: You don't want anything to make me as happy as you do. But if you're willing to chase this result by eliminating everything else I might love from my life, then I don't want you. Confidence to stand among the things I love is sexy; the opposite is the opposite.

If you try to separate me from my relationships, my priorities, or my comfort level about expressing my feelings, you might as well move on to someone who meets your standards.

An overwrought sense of urgency. Poker players are fond of saying that their game is just one long hand, and Man Code men view romance the same way. That's why we sweat the meaning of individual moments less and pay attention to general themes. Women tend to do the opposite. They sweat each hand like it's the last one they'll ever play. What does it mean that I went out with my friends that one night? What does it mean that I didn't call? What does it mean that I stayed late at work all week?

What it means is generally nothing. Ulterior motives are not a Man Code thing. Things are what they are.

What this signifies to us is an overall lack of appreciation. What a woman is saying is that all the things you've done for me in the past don't matter. This instant is what matters. As I've said before, Man Code men will do anything for you so long as you appreciate it. If you don't, it's over.

Why are women the ones men share with? Because ultimately, they're the ones who care, who nurture, who understand. But television and magazines are almost breeding this instinct out of women because they make you feel like there's something wrong with you if you're not married with children by 30, among other offenses. Women used to be the ones willing to wait, who were patient and understanding. Women need to get over this modern impression of what love looks like—

cute and willing to say anything, do anything, and/or say and do everything constantly (i.e., Jake Pavelka)—or they'll never get the authentic love they deserve.

Sex on the first date. See subsequent chapter titled, "Sex and the Man Code Man."

Talking things to death. Reality TV shows—including two to which I've contributed—are about a cartoon version of love. You meet, you go on perfect dates in perfect places with perfect-looking people, and throughout you have deep conversations that lead to an inevitable proposal. Let me tell you, there's a reason none of these engagements go the distance. It's because love needs momentum that can only be supplied by the two people involved. Once the cameras go away and it's just the two of you standing there trying to figure out how to make your schedules work or ends meet, all that talking you did on TV means nothing.

In reality, love is quiet. It's about silently lifting the rock together when you want to throw it at each other. It's what you do when no one is looking. It's about how you find the person's hand in the dark on the nights when things are really bad, telling the person it's OK.

As I say a lot in this book, Man Code men view talk as basic economics. If I start to tell you I love you constantly, complimenting you incessantly, it all loses its value. Love is the result of the events in our lives, not the result of talking about the idea of it.

True romance looks nothing like it does on these shows, where what is substituted is a "love" that is talked about and tortured to death.

Quiet does not mean disinterest. Man Code men simply believe you shouldn't talk unless you can improve the silence.

Disloyalty. As I've said before, loyalty is the currency of our lives. It's the thing we value most. I feel I won "Bachelor Pad" because I was loyal. Obviously, if you're disloyal to me somehow, that's horrible. But what's also unattractive is when women treat one another as sport. It turns my stomach to watch Woman 1 be sweet to Woman 2's face, then talk about Woman 2 as though she's a pro football team to Woman 3. If we see you being disloyal to other women, it signifies you'll be disloyal to us, too.

Eleanor Roosevelt said, "Great minds talk about ideas, average minds talk about events, and small minds talk about other people." Man Code men are looking for women who are great, not small.

A failure to let a lion be a lion. In today's world, men and women stand on equal ground, which is exactly as it should be. But sometimes a woman wants to be taken care of, protected and made to feel safe. Similarly, a Man Code man wants to be shown he's the one who made her feel that way. Inside, we're like lions promenading around with our chests out, heads up and knowing that we run this jungle—at least when we're at our best. Letting us know that we're succeeding in making you feel protected goes a long way. With a look or word, you can empower us.

David Good

WHAT MAN CODE MEN
ARE LOOKING FOR

We've established the following:

Things women must accept about Man Code Men.

Things Man Code men value.

The stumbling blocks Man Code men hit on the way to love.

Let's bring it home by being forward looking. Let's talk about what Man Code men are looking for in a partner. To us, it seems simple, but obviously isn't. (I know women say it all the time: "Why can't I just meet a man who..." Believe it or not, we say the same thing.)

I can tell you that the experiences I've had over the past couple years—being on shows that revolve around romance, and then being set free into the world with a lot more name recognition than I started with—have only heightened the way I feel on this topic.

I've talked a lot about how attractive confidence is in a woman, and I can tell you that a lady who doesn't need the job is the most likely to get it. That doesn't mean that we find arrogance or indifference attractive. Those are awful qualities.

But there is so much pressure exerted on women these days—by the media, by other women, by social networking, and of course by guys—to be in a relationship that they start to seek one indiscriminate of who the partner actually is. It's very hard to watch and sad, and Man Code men are seeking women with the wisdom to see beyond all that. Why would they want a bad boy if he's, you know, bad? Why would they want to exert energy on a bad relationship when they've got plenty of good ones with their friends and families? Why talk themselves into something they don't really want?

As I said, I've contributed to this by virtue of participating in shows that create an exaggerated perception of love. One thing that knocks me out about them is that one season, a person will be in the final running to win "the prize", i.e., getting engaged on "The Bachelor" or "Bachelorette." They profess their undying love, but unfortunately aren't the one picked in the end.

Let's put this in a real world context: You love someone with all your heart, but just as you think you might get engaged, he/she gets engaged to someone else. What? That would be beyond devastating, and that's why it makes great television.

Now here's the kicker: That same person who finished No. 2—who ostensibly should be just pulling his/her life together— is back on as "The Bachelorette" or "Bachelor" the next season saying the same things not one year later.

Again, great television. But it's all about winning; it's not about real romance. And when you're on the show, you know that. You suspend reality for a while because pride makes you go toward that goal, yet when you don't win it's something of a relief.

(Incidentally, I thought "Bachelor Pad" was great because it wasn't necessarily about dating. If a relationship sprang up, great, but it was more about the human dynamic of making our own goals co-exist with those of others'. That's a lot like work, teams and similar group environments. Obviously the romantic attachments keep the audience interested, but that's not the end goal.)

When you're on these shows, you concede to the plotline, but in your heart you know it's all a little false. But the audience of 15 million does not know this, and the result is the same sense of urgency about finding a mate becoming a self-fulfilling prophecy. Man Code men are looking for someone without this air of desperation.

This being said, in no particular order, here are some other things we're seeking in a partner:

- ☑ She makes eye contact when you first meet.
- ☑ She's a natural beauty.
- ☑ She has some sort of core conviction about what she wants in life and what she doesn't want.
- ☑ She's as conscious of the needs of others as she is of her own.
- ☑ She's independent.
- ☑ She's lets her partner know he's succeeding. (In their quest to be complimented, my experience is that women forget to compliment men. Man Code men are driven, competitive, ego-bound individuals. So long as the compliment is genuine, if you have a positive thought about your Man Code man, say it. Good men should be told they're good men. Dishonorable men should just be left alone.)
- ☑ She'll also tell us when we're failing, if we actually are.
- ☑ She'll drink with us, but not more than us.
- ☑ She gets the joke.
- ☑ She's motivated.
- ☑ She has good morals.
- ☑ She's consistent.
- ☑ She doesn't put streaks in or otherwise screw up her hair. No old-lady hair.
- ☑ She does not talk about our relationship to her friends more than she talks about it to us.
- ☑ She puts family at the center of her life.
- ☑ She can contribute in a social setting rather than just be arm candy.
- ☑ She can tell a story.
- ☑ She's not hung up on the way things look. She can sit at the bar and have dinner if there are no tables. She's not prone to spending needlessly on things that will impress her friends but mean nothing in the end.
- ☑ She's not a doormat.

☑ She cooks for us. (But expects us to cook for her, too.)
☑ She's OK with the fact that sometimes we're not thinking about her.
☑ She has her own life.
☑ She has her own career and her own money.
☑ She can change our minds. (I personally love discourse. I'm dying to have my mind changed, though my friends who know me as being damn stubborn would probably disagree. But good-natured disagreement is the spice of life.)

What I hope you take from this is that we want you to value yourself first and foremost. We don't want you to feel like you must value us first and only. You are not a supporting player in our lives. My goal in making this list is that you see we don't want you to be some contrivance. We want you to be you, and like being you. We respond to that.

In short, what a Man Code Man responds to is a woman who has her own code.

David Good

SEX AND THE MAN CODE MAN

When it comes to sex, there is a double standard that may be unfortunate but is true. While Man Code men believe in chivalry, we're also red-blooded and carnal, like all guys. We're sexual creatures. If we are unattached, and if you are an attractive woman who offers us sex on the first date, we will probably take you up on it. (The only exceptions are religious men—and I mean, REALLY devoted religious men.)

But we won't marry you. That is a virtual lock.

This isn't to say that we'll test you. I can say with a clear conscience that I've never tested a woman by coming on to her, hoping she'll say no. What I do find extremely attractive is a woman who feels confident enough to not feel a need to "close the deal" by us getting into bed.

Nothing is as cool as a woman who's poised enough to give you a kiss and then heads upstairs saying, "Talk to you tomorrow." Having been in relationships of nine and four years, I can say that monogamous sex exceeds all other forms. I might need to go home and take a cold shower, but I'll also know that not having sex on the first date is ironically a great first step toward the best sex I'll ever have.

Confidence is unbelievably sexy. Desperation, a willingness to be flexible on your morals, and giving us the sense that you're breathlessly trying to fill the position of "boyfriend" so you can check "In a relationship" on your Facebook status—these are all immensely unattractive long term.

This is not to say that we won't have sex with you if we find you physically attractive. At its most fundamental, least emotional level, this is what men think about sex: It's a pleasurable activity and a biological function, like eating. If you offer unencumbered sex to a man, it's like giving him a free brownie. We are biologically oriented toward accepting it. This is hardware, not software.

But things won't get too much further, because you've set yourself up against some pretty insurmountable odds. If a woman is bringing me to bed after Date 1, I'm asking myself, "Is this a woman I want raising my children; setting an example for my daughters? Um, no."

Contrary to what movies, TV shows and Maxim covers convey to women, we guys can exist without sex. We are not manic fiends at the mercy of our impulses. We're not just running around looking for outlets to plug into. She might be scorching hot, but nothing can overcome the astonishing unpleasantness of a woman with nothing to say.

Whatever happened to dating, anyway? I like dating. I love the pursuit, the chase. Anybody can have sex. But hanging on for four, five, six dates makes it that much better once it happens. In the back of my head, I want the story I tell my kids about my first date with their mom to be a good one. I don't want have to hide a thing. Conversely, "I met her in a bar, we got wasted, and then we went back to my place," is not that story.

I'm jealous that our parents got to date, where the guy drove over to the girl's parent's house, looked the dad in the eye and shook his hand. It's also a great forum for you to learn about us: our manners, chivalry, interests and goals. You get to see the tough-guy layers peeled away, unlike in a bar where all you see is what we're like when we're drunk and with our friends. You get to see if he pays, if he makes the phone call the day after, etc.

There's nothing wrong with having needs. We all do. That's why we date. We feel incomplete alone. Finding out if we can fill those needs long term is part of a great journey.

One of the coolest, most intimate moments I had with a woman actually occurred when we were filming "Bachelor Pad." I say this because in the throes of this great conversation, I forgot the cameras were there entirely, which is nearly impossible. And it all came courtesy of our winning a water-balloon toss, of all things.

Natalie and I won a competition where we had to toss water balloons to one another over greater and greater distances. For our victory, we got to drive a Lamborghini like we stole it down the Pacific Coast Highway to a totally private retreat. Once there, we made some drinks and sat down on the couch, where we got to talking about what we'd do if we won the final $250,000 prize.

Natalie said she'd pay off her student loans, and then do something for her family, to whom she was grateful because she'd come from " a long line of love." This led me to talking about how my parents' divorce affected me, and what a daddy's boy I was growing up. She said I should call my dad, and I told her I couldn't because we'd had a terrible fight before I left to do the show. (By the time the show aired, my dad and I had cleared the air and we're great now.) We talked until I didn't want to anymore, and then we stopped.

What was a four-minute clip on the show was actually a two-hour conversation in real life. When she wasn't speaking, Natalie was listening intently, asking great questions, and showed me some genuine wisdom. She wasn't weighing and measuring the conversation for what it meant in the grand scheme of our relationship. She wasn't strangling it to death. She valued my outpouring of emotion because I don't do it often. It's basic economics: the less there is of something, the more its worth, and she knew that. This would never have happened with a lot of women. It wasn't about what it meant; it was about just telling the truth. As the cameras cut away and she laid in my arms on the couch, you could see tears in my eyes. She put her head on my shoulder and no other words needed to be spoken. That was true intimacy coming from a great conversation, and it all happened fully clothed.

Here's a key insight when in the early stages of dating a Man Code man. We are ego-driven and therefore competitive. We also are considering you as the woman who will raise our kids. So when conversation runs out, do not under any circumstance default to telling us about your romantic past, particularly your racy romantic past. Absolutely zero can be gained from that, aside from you telling us that you did not have sex with someone we think you did. (You should hold us to not aimlessly disclosing this same sort of information.) Again, you are only scrambling the wiring. This might not be a fair standard, but when it comes to sex, we're talking about impulses, not reason. I can tell you with absolute confidence that maintaining some mystery along these lines benefits everyone.

Once restraint gives way to some hard-earned sex, you should know that once the emotional groundwork is laid, we really like it when you initiate sex. Unlike the Date 1 axiom, your initiating sex down the line gives us immense confidence and makes you incredibly alluring. We love the chase, but after we've caught you, it's cool if you take lead once in a while. When in doubt, the best last-minute gift is you in lingerie.

So, let's review: At the end of that first date, if you like him, give him a kiss. A real one, and leave him wanting more. But give it to him in one shot, and that's it. Chase is done, race is won, next...kiss him, kiss him good, and you've got him hooked—if he's a real Man Code man, that is.

David Good

HOW TO RAISE A
MAN CODE MAN

As I asserted earlier in this book, because of divorce, roughly two-thirds of boys in America are being raised in households where a father is not present daily. With increased frequency, boys are making their man code out of whole cloth. They don't know what's real and what's imagined, and what emerges is a cartoon version of masculinity.

Can a Man Code man be raised in such an environment? Absolutely. I am Exhibit A.

My parents divorced when I was nine, and initially I only saw my father once every two weeks. My mother's great wisdom was such that even though there was sadness and resentment between her and my father, she knew I needed him to become a strong man in the world, and so she always encouraged our spending time together. She was not concerned with appearing the victor at my expense, for that would not have truly been winning, and she knew that. I've known a lot of guys whose moms used them as collateral in a divorce, but mine never did that.

In the same vein, because I did not have a man in the home to show me every day how to behave, she was extremely literal in telling me how I must treat women. She told me exactly what she expected of me, and she never brought a man into my life that was anything less than what she described. She never allowed men to treat her as a lesser being. In short, she knew

I was watching and learning despite it being a less than ideal classroom on the surface, and she made the best of it.

I know that she, like other successful single moms, had to overcome some base maternal instincts, namely to protect my feelings. Mothers are nurturers and defenders of their children's psyches. Moms prop us up; Dads show us how to get up four times if we've been knocked down three. There's a reason why dads are the ones to teach us to ride our bikes and put our heads underwater: they're willing to be unpopular if momentary misery gets us to the promised land eventually.

Mothers want us to be happy all the time, but the reality is that feelings need to be hurt if we're to grow. My mom allowed me to compete, to challenge myself, and she never allowed me to fear failure.

The best lessons in a boy's life often come in the form of an old-school knockdown. It's just this sort of tail-kicking that adjusts our attitude and steels our resolve. Moms can't teach us everything; sometimes you have to stand aside and let life take a turn.

Again, I am not an expert in anything but Man Code, and I can tell you that based on my experience, Man Code men have some common denominators in their upbringings:

Loyalty. Be it loyalty to a team or a friend, the theme is encouraged through times high and low. Boys who are taught to sell low on their friends and family become loyal only to themselves.

Hard work. For some reason, we're seeing the death of the summer job, which I think is essential. Whatever the avocation—be it school, sports or a job—a boy needs to learn to take the dirt road. This often involves discomfort and misery, two things our moms instinctively defend us from. But there is one unassailable fact of life, and that is a man dignifies himself by working. If a guy's not taught this early on, he'll be doomed to an undignified life.

Competition. This is a big one. As a society, we've come to prioritize equal outcome over equal opportunity, and I think this has to do with the absence of our fathers. All a man should want in life is a chance, and when he gets it, he needs to take it. Sports are certainly an elevated form of competition, but not the only form. Your boy might be an actor or an obo player. It really doesn't matter the form it takes. Some day, he's going to be up against someone else for that lead role or that orchestra seat, and you better hope he's got his big-boy pants on when he does. Competing is its own skill, and if a boy doesn't have it, life is going to be pretty average. Notice I didn't say that "winning" is a skill. That would be prioritizing the outcome. Let your kid lose. It'll put hair on his chest and let him know he can take a punch.

Leaving the nest. This is a really hard one for moms, for the nest is their creation. I get it, I really do: You spend 18 years building a place of unconditional love. It's totally counterintuitive to tell your boy to leave. That's usually that dad's job. But he does need to go. Moms fear that their boys will find a place they love more than home, or they're afraid they won't, or both. It's all well-meaning, but you have to let your kid have that journey.

The ability to socialize. I fear for our generation of shut-ins, video gamers and texters who don't know how to sit at a dinner table and talk. I wonder if there will come a day when Congress just checks in from their beanbag chairs. Your kid needs to socialize, and he needs to do it outside. If your boy only knows how to shoot baskets, make music or have a conversation online, he will turn into one big boorish drone. That is a fact.

Team. Every successful person I know is familiar with the inner-workings of a team. Again, this doesn't have to be sports. He can be on the math team. The point is he needs to know how to find his place in a larger whole, to make his personal goals part of the group's. A family is a team, and if your boy is going to lead a family, he needs to have been there before.

Tough love. What good is a rule if it can be broken without the threat of punishment? If your kid makes a mess, he needs to own the mess. Do not defend him reflexively. If his coach comes to you and says, "Johnny broke this rule. He's suspended from the team," you need to say, "I'll take it from here, Coach," not "That's impossible, my son would never do that."

Accountability. Guys these days are increasingly entitled. They think the world owes them happiness, which they should access any time they want. If your kid is the sort who takes every sick day and uses all his "flex time," he is destined to be Employee No. 1009 for the rest of his natural-born days. Your kid is not owed an improved lot in life. If he wants it, guess what? It's on him.

Pride. Your boy has to be taught the concept of pride in his work, his team, his last name and his country. He needs to know he's part of a larger fabric, and that a standard has been set that he needs to carry on. We live in a great country. Your boy has a chance for a great life, but is not entitled to that chance. He needs to stand for something. If you're woman enough to raise a man, he'll know just what he's standing for.

David Good

CONCLUSION

Where do we go from here? Hopefully this look under the hood has been in some way insightful. My goal with this book has been to do my small part for both men and women to foster a little mutual understanding. Moreover, I suppose that by helping women know Man Code men, they'll help perpetuate the species. As I say in Chapter 3, I feel our herd is thinning, with momentum going in the wrong direction. The only way Man Code men can persist is if women insist on being with only the best of us. No more "filling the position." It's time for ladies to hold out for something great, which they deserve.

In terms of understanding Man Code men, an important takeaway is that we would rather not be loved at all than feel the rules we live by are somehow inadequate or not worthy of respect. We are this way to a fault. Women are somewhat the opposite in that the act of being in a relationship tends to be as valuable as the relationship itself. They want the relationship to have the aesthetic components of a relationship as much or more than they want it to have real soul. I mean, ultimately they want that true meaning, but often give up the best years of their lives hoping the relationship they're in will become meaningful. I imagine a lot of this has to do with a woman's biological clock, and that having a finite number of child-baring years makes the cost of breaking up and starting over costly.

I suppose what I mean by all this is that Man Code men take that sense of belonging overly seriously, while women might not take it seriously enough.

Be this as it may, I want you to know that what Man Code men are after is not a prettier girl, a more seductive girl or a more permissive girl. We do want soul. We do want someone with the same sort of core conviction we have.

When you believe in yourself, your belief in us takes on an elevated meaning. We want and need to know that you respect us privately and publicly. Man Code men thrive when they know that their ladies trust them, admire them, and believe in them. Men are driven by respect and admiration, and by this I don't simply mean that we want to be respected and admired—we also want to respect and admire you.

Much as I want women to find love, I also want them to feel loved. Man Code men show our affection and admiration poorly oftentimes. But it's there. I think I also want you to know that, even though we show it poorly. Part of my writing this book is that we're showing you that we love you more than you probably realize. We get frustrated when you ask for more expression because we feel that we already are showing you.

Remember that Man Code men are conquerors and providers, which is an expression of his love to his woman, by providing a home, a car, money for food and bills, etc. We just want women to understand this and acknowledge their appreciation of these deeds. Intellectually, it doesn't matter how much income a man makes, or whether or not his wife makes more or less money in her career. But Man Code men innately bear the emotional burden of being the provider. It is not a choice; It is never far from our minds and can sometimes make us feel overwhelmed.

I hope that if nothing else, women walk away from this book inspired and empowered, not just by an understanding of what Man Code men want, but also by the knowledge that what we want is the real you. I fear that women increasingly feel like failures if they don't have a man, and therefore are willing to become some contrivance of their real persona in order to land us.

Nothing could be further from what we want. It comes down to soulfulness. Do you have it, and can we have it together?

ABOUT THE AUTHOR

David Good was born and raised in West Alexandria, Ohio, a community with just 1,500 people. There were just 93 students in his class when he graduated from Twin Valley South High School.

A born entrepreneur like his father, David originally went to work as a broker for a truckload freight company, first in Cincinnati and later in Tampa, Fla. After a period with the family business in Camden, he moved on to found Man Code brand.

David gained national notoriety in 2009 when he appeared on "The Bachelorette: Season 5" (Jillian's season). On the show, he won the first-impression rose. Among all the male contestants, David was chosen by the Harlem Globetrotters to play on their team for a day.

In 2010, he joined 20 past "Bachelor" and "Bachelorette" contestants on "Bachelor Pad." The participants were united under one roof in a competitive reality series to compete for $250,000. David and partner Natalie Getz ultimately won the competition, splitting the grand prize.

Today, David travels around the country in support of his new book, "The Man Code." He's proud that some proceeds from the book go to cancer research. He lives in Tampa.

FOLLOW DAVID GOOD

Please continue to follow David Good:

Website
www.ManCodeBook.com

 Facebook
www.facebook.com/ManCodeBook

 Twitter
www.twitter.com/DaveLGood